DUE DATE

Everything You Need To Know About

TEEN
FATHERHOOD

Fatherhood brings both extra responsibilities and new joys.

• THE NEED TO KNOW LIBRARY •

Everything You Need To Know About

TEEN FATHERHOOD

Eleanor H. Ayer

THE ROSEN PUBLISHING GROUP, INC.
NEW YORK

Published in 1993 by The Rosen Publishing Group, Inc.
29 East 21st Street, New York, NY 10010

First Edition
Copyright © 1993 by The Rosen Publishing Group, Inc.

Manufactured in the United States of America.

Library of Congress Cataloging-in-Publication Data

Ayer, Eleanor H.
    Everything you need to know about teen fatherhood / Eleanor H.
Ayer. — 1st ed.
    (The Need to know library)
    Includes bibliographical references and index.
    Summary: Discusses the emotional, physical, and financial con-
cerns involved with becoming a teenage father and examines the
responsibilities and choices offered by the situation.
    ISBN 0-8239-1532-8
    1. Teenage fathers—United States—Juvenile Literature. 2. Teenage
fathers—United States—Life skills guides—Juvenile literature. 3.
Unmarried fathers—United States—Juvenile literature. [1. Teenage
fathers.] I. Title.
HQ756.7.A94 1993
306.874'2'0835—dc20   92-39945
                                            CIP
                                            AC

Contents

Introduction: Before You Become a Father

For many teens, being in love is like feeling fire and ice at the same time. It's good and it's bad. It's exciting and it's scary. But mostly, it's confusing.

Does this sound familiar? You meet a girl you really like. You begin dating. You spend more and more time together. You want to know this person better. You want to show her how you feel. And you want to know how she feels about you.

What If?

You may want to have a sexual relationship with someone special, but you're not sure. It would be wonderful to be so close. But what if she gets *pregnant*? What will you do?

If you're old enough to have *intercourse* (sex), you're old enough to act responsibly. A girl can become pregnant the very first time she has sex. Think seriously about this *before* you begin your relationship. Ask yourself, "Am I really ready to change my life and become a father? Am I ready to make a *commitment* to raising a child?"

Becoming a father is not the only way your life may be changed by having sex. Today, the threat of *AIDS* is greater than ever. This deadly disease prevents your body's *immune system* from fighting illness. You can get AIDS when you have sex with a person who is infected. It takes only one time. At present, there is no cure for AIDS. All people who have it die early deaths. AIDS is the most serious of all sexually transmitted diseases, but it is not the only one. You can also get *syphilis, gonorrhea, genital herpes*, and other diseases.

Protecting Yourself and Your Girlfriend

The thought of getting AIDS or another sexual disease is frightening. The thought of fatherhood can also be frightening. But there are ways to protect yourself and your girlfriend.

The surest way is *abstinence*—avoid having sex altogether. Stay away from situations that make having sex easy or inviting.

- Date with other couples or in groups.
- Don't stay with your girlfriend in a car or house when no one else is there.

- Avoid long sessions of kissing or touching each other.
- Decide in advance with your girlfriend that sex will not be part of your relationship unless you are married. Having a clear understanding beforehand will make it easier to abstain.

If you feel that abstinence is not possible, you will need to practice "safe sex." Safe sex is low-risk sex. Using a *condom*, a rubber casing rolled over an erect penis, offers two kinds of protection. A condom may be used to prevent an unwanted pregnancy, and also to reduce the risk of infection from STDs (sexually transmitted diseases).

The Importance of Talking and Reading

Both you and your girlfriend must be responsible for your actions. You have choices to make. Talk to each other. Take time to think things through.

To make the important decision about becoming a father, you need to talk to others besides your girlfriend. Try talking with your parents. What is it *really* like to raise a child? How will it change your life? Listen to people who became fathers when they were teenagers. Are they glad they did it? Do they have any regrets? What were the hard times like?

Talk with your school counselor or religious leader. If you feel uncomfortable talking to someone you know, try an outside agency like Planned

Couples need to act responsibly about decisions that
involve sex.

Parenthood. Trained counselors can discuss your
feelings and answer your questions. They can help
you to make wise choices about sex. Some helpful
agencies are listed in the back of this book.

Don't just talk. Read. There are many books
about teen fatherhood available. There are also
videos and magazine articles. Your local librarian
can help. Reading gives you a chance to think. It
can help you to make up your own mind. Gather all
the information you can. Becoming a father is an
important step for you, for your partner, and for the
child. Make sure you are prepared.

Talking to parents may be helpful in reaching a decision about an unexpected pregnancy.

Chapter 1

Discovering You're a Father

*D*ave *was delighted when he heard the news. He and his girlfriend had been dating six months. They were making plans to get married after high school. Now that Sarah was pregnant, they would get married sooner.*

José was 17 at the time. He had been dating Angela for a couple of months. They spent a lot of time together. Maybe too much. When Angela told José she was pregnant, he left. "I couldn't handle it," he later admitted. " I had to get away. My dad was living in a different town, so I went to stay with him."

Confusing Feelings

People react in different ways to the news about a pregnancy. Some common feelings are:

Shock The news comes as a total surprise. You never dreamed it would happen to you. You're not sure what you will do now.

Anger You're very upset. You knew it could happen, but you're angry just the same. Perhaps you blame your girlfriend for not using some kind of birth control. Or maybe you blame yourself for not being more careful.

Denial You refuse to believe the news. There must be some mistake. "If I ignore this, it will go away," you tell yourself.

Fear You're scared. How will your parents and her parents take the news? Will they help you or hate you? What will your friends say? How will you support this child? Who will raise it?

Acceptance OK. You weren't really ready to be a father. You didn't want your girlfriend to get pregnant right now. But it's happened. You accept it. The two of you talk to your parents and decide what to do.

Joy You're delighted! You and your girlfriend had been thinking about marriage. Now you have a good reason to start planning a life together.

Facing Facts with Your Girlfriend

Perhaps you and your girlfriend talked about having a family. Or maybe you were never that serious and didn't give the future much thought. Either way, news of the pregnancy can change your relationship. If you discussed pregnancy beforehand and made plans, it could be easier for both of you now.

Jake and Amy had never talked about kids. "It sounds crazy," Jake said, "but I didn't feel I knew her well enough to talk about marriage or babies. We'd only been dating a few weeks."

But things happened too fast for Jake and Amy. They weren't prepared for the news that Amy was pregnant. "We had to ask ourselves if we wanted to spend the rest of our lives together," Jake continued. "That really opened our eyes. Amy was hysterical, and I was pretty close to the edge myself." Amy and Jake's parents helped them decide what to do. Amy would go to the family-planning clinic and talk to a counselor about ending her pregnancy.

Even if you think you know what you want, the reality of pregnancy can sometimes change your mind.

Darian knew Shawna wanted a baby. Three of her friends had babies that they brought to school. She thought they were really cute. "I told her if she wanted to get pregnant, it was OK with me," Darian said, " so long as she didn't mind raising the kid herself. I didn't want any part of it."

That was the plan—until Shawna got pregnant. Then Darian realized, "This is going to be my child, too. I pictured him or her calling someone else 'Daddy,' and it just changed my whole way of thinking. I wanted this kid in my life."

Telling the Family

Once you and your girlfriend have adjusted to the news, it's time to tell your parents. There's no easy way. Even if both of you are happy about the pregnancy, it still can be uncomfortable to talk about. It's usually better that your parents hear the news from you. It can be more upsetting if they are told by someone outside the family.

Being honest will make the situation easier. You may be happy or frightened to hear that you have fathered a child. Like José, you may want to run. Or like Dave, you may be proud. No matter how you feel, be honest.

Not all parents will be calm and helpful. Some will be angry, some will be hurt, and some will treat you like a child who's not able to make his own decisions. Wilt's parents were understanding, but his girlfriend's were not. "They treated me like dirt," Wilt told a friend. "They wanted me out of the picture completely. All they could think about was protecting their little girl. 'But, hey,' I told them. 'We're in this together.' That didn't seem to matter."

You Have the Power to Direct Your Own Life

As an older teen, you should have a voice in making decisions that will affect your life. It's always wise to listen to other responsible adults, but your opinion is important, too.

You may be your own best judge. You know what you *can* do and what you *will* do better than anyone else. Be honest with yourself. If you think you are ready to raise your child, be firm with those who disagree. If you think you are not ready to be a good parent, admit it. Work with your family, your girlfriend, and your social worker to find another way to handle things.

Jolene and Francisco hadn't planned on pregnancy. But now, with a baby on the way, they decided to get married. "Our parents thought we were nuts," recalled Francisco. "They tried to stop us. Jolene said she'd run away if she had to. But we wanted to keep peace in the family if we could."

The couple made plans. They talked with their parents about where they would live, where Francisco would work, and how much money he could make. Jolene told how she planned to finish school and take care of the baby at the same time. When their parents heard them trying to work things out, they began treating them more like adults.

One of the good things about acting like an adult is having more control over your life. You make the decisions that affect you. But with that control comes responsibility. You must stand behind your actions. The decisions you make won't always be right. Your choices may sometimes be foolish. You can learn from your mistakes. But *you* must take the responsibility for them.

Chapter 2

Deciding What's Right for You

Years ago, when a boy got a girl pregnant, there was only one choice: marriage. People thought marriage was "the only honorable thing to do." Today there are other options. Marriage is no longer the only answer to pregnancy.

Considering Abortion

If the pregnancy was unplanned and you have no desire or ability to raise a child, *abortion* may be a choice. It is a quick way to end a pregnancy. It is the choice of many teens who feel they are not ready to be parents. But abortion is a serious and difficult decision. It should not be thought of as a form of birth control. Abortion means choosing not to bring a child into the world. This is a memory that will stay with you forever.

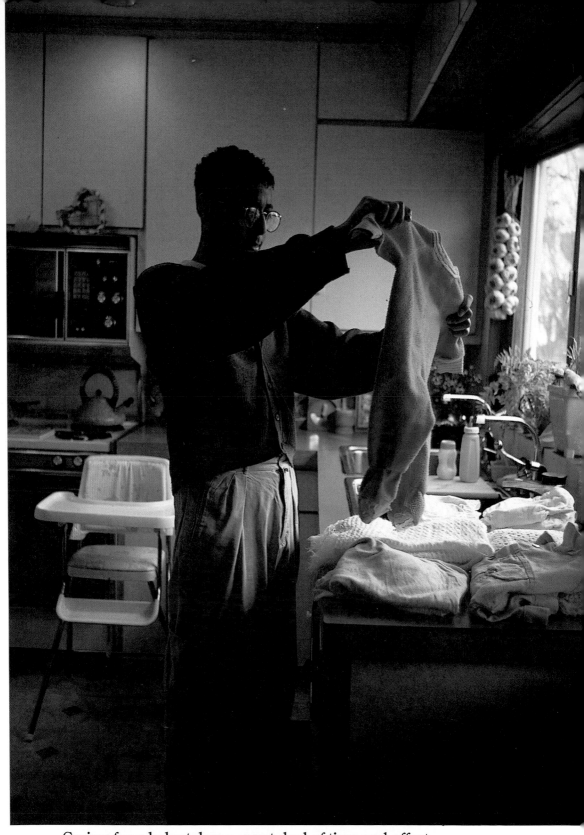

Caring for a baby takes a great deal of time and effort.

During the first three months of pregnancy, the girl and her family may choose abortion even if the father does not agree. It is the woman's decision. Later in the pregnancy, when abortion is more dangerous to the mother's health, the doctor or even the state may get involved in the decision. Abortion restrictions differ from state to state.

Adoption

Many teens who are against abortion but are not ready or able to raise their children, choose *adoption*. "We wanted him to have a chance to grow up, but we knew we couldn't give him a good home. There are lots of couples waiting to adopt, so we figured he'd have a good chance," said one teen father.

Adoption, too, is often painful. "I was glad to have it all behind me," recalls Dan, who was 17 when he became a father. That was 20 years ago. "I'm glad I did what I did at the time, but it haunts me to think that I have a 20-year-old daughter out there somewhere."

In some states, a father has equal rights with a mother in deciding on adoption. In other states, the father has no say.   Check with your local social services office to find out about your rights.

There are many things you must consider if you are helping to make the adoption decision :

Adoption agencies If adoption is your choice but you don't know where to begin, look in the yellow pages under "Adoption Agencies." People at the agencies know the laws about adoption for your state. They know families who want to adopt a baby and would make good parents. They can help you through the difficult legal and personal steps involved in adoption.

To be sure that you're working with a good agency, check with a social worker. Call more than one agency. Find out how long each has been in business. Ask to see proof that they are licensed by the state.

Private adoption You or your religious advisor may know of a couple who would like to adopt your baby. In this case, you do not have to go through an agency. If a private adoption is your choice, be sure you work with a reputable lawyer to draw up the proper legal papers.

Signing the papers During pregnancy, you or your girlfriend may change your mind about adoption. This is normal. You can wait until the baby is born to sign the adoption papers. Adoption is not final until the papers are signed.

Knowing what you want You may be under pressure from parents, counselors, or even the adoption agency to give up your baby. But you and your girlfriend are the ones who must make the decision. No one else should decide for you.

Adoption is a very tough decision. If you use an agency, you probably will never see your baby after it is born. You will not know who the adopting

It is important to discuss adoption with people who are informed about all the different aspects.

parents are. This is done to protect their privacy as well as the child's. After the adoption is final, there is no going back. All your life you may wonder if you did the right thing. That is why it is so important to take your time and make your decision carefully. Find out all the facts. Talk with as many people as you can. Then trust in yourself that you will make the right decision.

When Marriage Is Your Choice

When Rick and Jennifer learned they were going to have a baby, they made the decision to get married. "We were happy, but very scared. We were against abortion. Both of us wanted to be with the child. At the time," recalled Rick, "I thought that was the right decision. Still I was worried. I didn't know how we were going to make it." Looking back, Rick admits he would do things differently.

Teen marriage is usually tense and stressful. Lack of money, job skills, and education can bring problems to a marriage. So can the pressure to be a good parent and father. Many teen marriages are not able to survive this stress, and the rate of divorce for teens is very high. A girl married at 17 is twice as likely to be divorced as a girl of 18 or 19. If she waits until 25, the chances that her marriage will last are four times better.

Living Together/Living Apart

Perhaps the idea of fatherhood is exciting, but the idea of marriage is not. You and your girlfriend may choose to have the baby but not to marry. You may decide to live together without being married, or live apart and share the responsibility of raising your child.

On the plus side, you can become a father without the pressure of becoming a husband at the same time. You can help raise your child and watch it grow and develop.

On the minus side, you have made no commitment to the child's mother. She has made none to you. Either of you could walk away at any time.

If you are not married, you must be sure that your rights as a father are protected. In many states, your name will not appear on the child's birth certificate unless the mother requests it. If you want to be named legally as the father, you must have a *paternity test*. If the test is positive, you may be the father and your name may be added to the birth certificate. This gives you legal rights to your child.

The legal father, however, must pay child support even if he has never been married to the mother. Child support begins when the baby is born and usually continues until he or she is 18. Even if the father is still in school, he must make child support payments. The court may require him to make only part of each payment. But he has to pay the rest as soon as he is able.

Father as a Single Parent

Choosing to raise a baby alone is a choice very few teen fathers make. But it may be the right choice for you. Being "Mr. Mom" will not be easy, but it can be very rewarding. Before you make your decision, ask yourself these questions:

- Do you *want* to learn how to care for a baby?
- Can you handle the double load of working and being a full-time single parent?

- Who will care for the child while you are away from the home ?
- What kind of support can you expect from the mother?
- Are you ready to make this important lifetime commitment?
- What if your girlfriend comes back in a year and wants to take the child? How can you be sure you and the child are protected?

The Decision Is Yours

Whatever your choice, it must be the one that you think is right. If you do not feel good about your decision, time will only make it worse. Talk with many people. Try to find an older man who became a father as a teenager.   See how it worked for him. How does he feel now about the decision he made as a teen?

Counselors at schools, churches, hospitals, and social services agencies are trained to help young people solve difficult problems.

Try to listen to your parents or older family members, too. Even if the pregnancy has made them angry, they can be helpful. Age and experience help people to make better decisions. Your parents know you well. They may surprise you by offering some very good advice.

It may be necessary to get a full-time or part-time job in order to fulfill the responsibilities of fatherhood.

Chapter 3

Growing Up on Fast Forward

Becoming a teenage dad means growing up in a big hurry. Suddenly, you face a huge responsibility. Just 10 years ago, you were a little child yourself. You needed a safe home where people loved you. You needed clean clothes and nourishing food. You needed guidance to grow up to be a good person. Now you must provide those things for your own child.

A Question of Paternity

Sometimes there is a reason to question who is the baby's father. It was that way with José and Angela. "That's one reason I ran," José admits. "Sure, Angela and I had been having sex. But I know she had been with other guys, too. One of them could have been the father."

José got scared when Angela started pressing him to marry her. "She told me that even if I didn't, I still had to pay child support for the next 18 years. I didn't even have a job. I panicked."

A paternity test could have helped José answer the question of fatherhood. This is a medical test in which blood from the mother, the father, and the baby are compared. If the test is negative, it shows that this man could not have been the baby's father. If the test is positive, it does not prove that he *is* the father. Only that he *might* be. It is possible to have a paternity test before the baby is born, but this is much more expensive. If there is any question in your mind that you might not be the father, you will want to have a paternity test. A doctor or clinic can tell you how to arrange for it.

Accepting Your Responsibility

When you choose to raise your baby, you make a commitment. You promise to give the child love, guidance, money, and a good home for nearly 18 years. You promise to raise your child in the very best way you can. There's no backing out of fatherhood.

Accepting such a big responsibility can make you scared and uncertain. This is natural. But you are not alone. Your girlfriend is probably just as scared and uncertain as you are. She needs your *moral support* right now, and you need hers. If raising your child is your choice, you must both

make the commitment to do a good job. Being
a good dad is just as big a responsibility as being a
good mom.

You're Not Alone

Teen pregnancy is on the rise. From 1940 to
1980, the number of teenagers having babies
tripled. The number of young, unmarried couples
living together in the 1990s is eight times greater
than it was in 1970. Today, more than one out of
every three boys is sexually active by the age of 15.

Becoming sexually active means facing the fact
that you may become a father. Teenage boys are
now responsible for 1.1 million pregnancies each
year. Yet fewer than half of those who become
fathers actually continue to support their children.
Only 10 percent (1 out of 10) marry, and usually
the marriages don't last long.

These statistics don't seem to paint a good picture of teen fatherhood. Yet some people, like
Dave, may be an exception. Now 33, Dave has no
regrets about having become a teen father. "When
you have your children early, you have the energy
to play with them and do things with them that you
don't as an older adult. When you're young, your
career isn't such a big part of your life. You have
more time to spend with the family." Looking back
after 15 years, Dave says, "I have no complaints. If
I had it to do over again, I would do things the
same way."

Regular visits to the doctor are important during pregnancy.

Chapter 4

Preparing for Childbirth

A normal pregnancy usually lasts for nine months. Most people need that long to adjust to the idea of parenthood. As a future father, you may need to think about practical things like getting a job, making a *budget*, fixing up baby's room, and just finding the time to be a dad.

Mom, meanwhile, is learning to adjust to her changing body. Every pregnancy is different. Some women feel very few side effects, others may feel sick or uncomfortable. There is no way to know in advance how a pregnancy will progress.

Prenatal Care

Every pregnant woman should get good prenatal (before birth) care. Without the proper care, the baby may be born with serious health problems. It may die during the first year.

29

Most doctors advise one checkup a month during the first seven months of pregnancy. In the eighth month, the mother should go every two weeks, and once a week during her last month. The father is welcome at all prenatal visits. You may have insurance to cover the cost of a private doctor. If not, check with your social services office to see about Medicaid or a low-cost clinic.

Good prenatal care means that the mother must eat a well-balanced diet and not harm her body in any way. As the father, you can help Mom follow some smart rules for pregnancy.

- Avoid gaining weight too quickly.
- Exercise regularly. A brisk walk or a swim several times a week may work out well.
- Never drink alcohol or use drugs. Even aspirin can cause harm to the unborn baby.
- Avoid drinks with caffeine, such as coffee, tea, and soda, whenever possible.
- No smoking!

The Three Stages of Pregnancy

If you divide the nine months of pregnancy by three, you have three *trimesters*, each three months long. During the first trimester, a woman may feel sick to her stomach much of the time. Foods that were once her favorites may seem disgusting to her now. Or she may get cravings for other foods. The changes going on in her body can cause heartburn, constipation, dizziness, or other symptoms.

Along with the changes in her body, you may notice changes in her moods. She may be happy one minute and crying the next. This is normal. She may be tired and irritable much of the time. Remember, pregnancy is not forever. Try to be patient.

During the second trimester, many women do not feel as sick or tired as they did earlier. The legs, breasts, and abdomen (belly) swell as the pregnancy begins to show. During this period, the *fetus*—the unborn baby—starts to move. You may occasionally feel this movement when you put your hand on the mother's abdomen. A doctor can hear the fetal heartbeat. By now the pregnancy is probably very real to both of you.

In the third trimester, the fetus may become quite active. All the extra weight may make the mother tire more easily. Routine jobs may be difficult for her. It is important for the mother's health and the baby's that she get a lot of rest during the last trimester.

As delivery day draws nearer, the mother may become worried. How painful is this going to be? Will the baby be OK? Am I ready to take my child home and care for it? Again, as father, your job is moral support. Try to understand how she feels. Let her know that she's not alone.

Although your own body has not changed during pregnancy, you may find that your moods are up and down, too. Try to relax. You can make it.

The Three Stages of Pregnancy

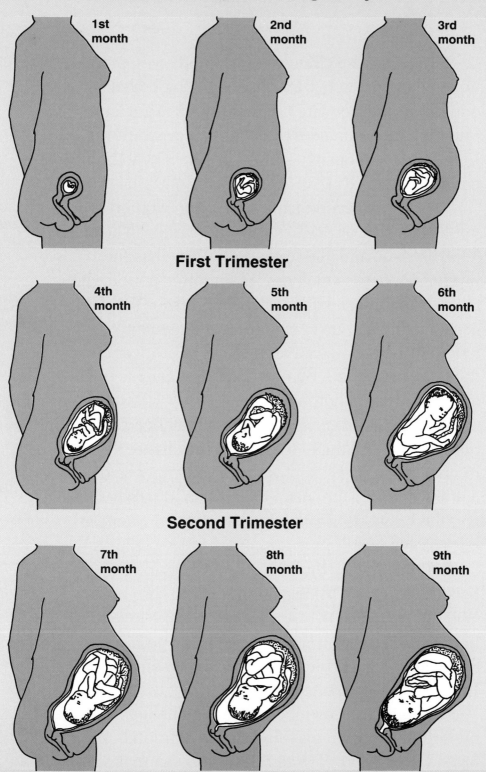

1st month

2nd month

3rd month

First Trimester

4th month

5th month

6th month

Second Trimester

7th month

8th month

9th month

Third Trimester

Getting Ready for the Big Day

Childbirth classes can help you prepare for *delivery*. Most hospitals or clinics offer classes to help both mother and father understand the process of pregnancy and childbirth.

You will learn about the different ways of having a baby. Perhaps you will decide to have your child at home, with the help of a *midwife*. This person is usually a woman. Although she is not a doctor, she is very experienced in delivering babies.

You may choose the *Lamaze* method of childbirth. This is a totally natural way of having a baby, without *anesthetics* or drugs. Both of you get involved in learning how the mother should breathe and push during delivery. Dad is the coach, helping Mom to relax and giving her encouragement. If Mom forgets how to breathe properly or when it's time to push, it's up to Dad to remind her. With the Lamaze method, you can have your baby in a hospital or at home.

Sometimes—depending on the health of the mother or the fetus—a *cesarean birth* may be necessary. This means the baby is delivered by surgery. A doctor performs an operation to remove the baby through a slit in the mother's abdomen. Some hospitals allow fathers to be in the operating room during this kind of birth.

If you think of any questions during the week, write them down. Your childbirth classes are prepared to discuss all of your concerns.

Keeping in touch with friends may help with the pressures of new responsibilities.

Chapter 5

Dealing with the Outside World

For Rick, the hardest part of becoming a father at 18 was "not being able to do things with my friends. I didn't have any time. I lost contact with them." Some expectant fathers work, some go to school, some do both. What little free time you have is usually spent with your girlfriend. There are many things you must do and talk about to prepare for a new baby.

You may also find that you have less in common with friends now. They probably have no idea what it's like to be an expectant father. They may not understand why you don't party as you used to. Even your best friend may suddenly seem childish and *immature* to you. You're headed in different directions. You are facing adult responsibility.

35

Juggling a Job

Whether or not you've ever had a job, it's time to get one now. Most teenagers can't count on their parents to support them and their new family. Your job may pay only *minimum wage* to start. That's okay. Most employers don't pay higher wages unless you have experience or an education. Chances are you have neither.

But you do have two things in your favor: a lot of energy, and a good reason to work. These are your strong points. Take advantage of them. Show your employer that you are willing to do more than is asked of you. Show him or her that you are eager to learn and improve in your job. Let your boss know that you have a family on the way and that you're trying your best to support it. If you show the boss that you're different, you will be treated differently. Soon you could be moving up the employment ladder—and up the pay scale.

If you're having trouble finding a job, don't get discouraged. Keep reading the classified ads and talking to people. Ask your school counselor for advice. Talk with a social worker. Go to the state unemployment office in your area. Sign up at a temporary service. Most local phone books list these agencies under "Employment" in the Yellow Pages. Even though millions of Americans are unemployed, there are usually jobs for people who are willing to start at the bottom, work hard, and improve.

Staying in School

Just because you have found a job doesn't mean you should quit school. It won't be easy, but *try to find a way to finish your education.* A high-school education is extremely important. Without one, it's much harder to find a good job and keep it.

It's easier to finish school before the baby is born. After that it's much harder to find the time (or a quiet place) to study. Perhaps you can work nights and go to school during the day. If not, look into *GED (General Equivalency Diploma)* classes at night. Your high school will have information.

Getting your high-school diploma will make you feel good about yourself. You'll be proud of having reached your goal. Your girlfriend will be proud of you, too. But most important, you'll be setting a good example for your child. By finishing school, you're showing your child that you think education is important. Your child will be much more likely to follow your example.

Handling All the Pressure

Pressure, commitments, responsibilities—how do you handle them all? Talking things over with a school social worker or counselor may help. If you are more comfortable talking with a family member or religious leader, that's fine, too. Most adults you trust will be glad to offer helpful ideas. And the more ideas you have, the better decisions you can make yourself.

A monthly budget gives you a sense of control over your finances.

Chapter 6

Balancing the Budget

As a responsible father, you should put your family's needs first. Money that is supposed to buy baby food cannot be spent on a new cassette tape. You must be sure that baby and mother have a secure place to live. This means paying the rent, heat, electric, and other important bills on time.

Even if you are not living together, you need to help support your child. The law says you must pay a certain portion of your child's bills. And as a good father, you should *want* to do this.

It's hard enough to support yourself. It's even harder when you're trying to support a child. How can you make ends meet? How do you know what to pay for first? By being very careful in the way you spend your money. You must make a plan—*a budget*—and follow that plan very closely.

Making Out a Budget

There are two sides to every budget: money that comes in and money that goes out. What comes in is your *income*. Income is any money you receive from wages, interest on an account, gifts, or other sources. What goes out are your *expenses*. This is the money you spend to pay the bills, start your savings, or buy the things you want.

How do you set up a budget? For many teens, a paycheck is the only income. But some have other sources. Your parents may help by lending you money. Perhaps you qualify for food stamps or other government programs. Make a list of all your income sources. Add up your monthly income from each source and write down the total.

Now list all your monthly expenses. You may want to use the sample budget on page 41 as a guide. *Be honest with yourself.* Don't leave off "Entertainment" if you *know* you're planning to go to the movies. If you're going to stick to your budget, it has to be truthful. Later you may decide to cut some expenses. But for now, list all of them.

When you have listed all your expenses, add up the total. How does it compare to your total income? If you have more expenses than income, it's time to make some choices. Decide which expenses are not really necessary. Instead of cutting out one whole section, try cutting down a little in several sections. The idea is to *balance the budget,* expenses matching income.

Setting a Little Aside

One of the most important parts of your budget is "Savings." Each month, set aside a regular amount of money for savings. It may be as little as $25. But try to save a regular amount *each month*. Increase that amount as often as you can. Never let savings be the item you cut out of your budget.

If you put your savings into a bank account, you won't be as tempted to spend it. When extra money is needed, work some overtime if you can. Do odd jobs for people. Draw money from savings only for emergencies.

Sample Monthly Budget

Income		Expenses	
Regular paychecks:	$____	Rent:	$____
Welfare or Social Services:	$____	Heat:	$____
Family contribution:	$____	Electricity:	$____
Other income:	$____	Water:	$____
		Phone:	$____
TOTAL INCOME:	$____	Food:	$____
		Clothing:	$____
		Health care:	$____
		Transportation:	$____
		Child care:	$____
		Entertainment:	$____
		Savings:	$____
		Other expenses:	$____
		TOTAL EXPENSES:	$____

What If You Still Can't Make It?

Rick and Jennifer tried their best. But there were times when they just couldn't make it. "Money was very tight," Rick remembers. What do you do when your income doesn't cover your expenses? How do you manage when you've cut everything out of the budget that you can?

"We had to borrow from Jennifer's mother once in a while," Rick recalls. "For a time, we had to live with her parents. Our apartment was too expensive. Those months were hard, but we were hopeful that better days would come."

While they were living with Jennifer's parents, Rick looked for a smaller apartment. He found one that was not as expensive as the first. Spending less on rent gave them more money to pay their other bills. "It took about six months for us to get back on our feet. But we did get there."

Don't be afraid to ask for help. It doesn't mean you're weak or that you're a failure. If you're working hard and trying your best, that's all you can do. In the meantime, don't be too proud. If there are people who are willing to help you, let them. Someday, you may be the one who can offer help to someone else.

Chapter 7

Bringing the Baby Home

"**P**roud" and "happy." Those are the words many teenage dads use when they talk about seeing their babies for the first time. If you stay with the mom during delivery, you may be the first to hold your baby after birth. This is a special time you will never forget.

Enjoy those few days in the hospital. It is a good time to become familiar with your new baby. You have lots of help around, too. Once baby comes home, he or she is all yours! There are no nurses to give bottles or change diapers. It's your job then—a job for you and Mom.

Paying for Baby's Birth

The cost of prenatal care and delivery can be very expensive. Find out well in advance of the baby's birth if you or your parents have health insurance. It is important to know what services are covered. In preparing your budget you'll need to know if you are paying all or part of the medical bills or just the cost of the insurance itself.

Most births are normal, without problems for mother or baby. Hospital stays are usually two or three days. But sometimes delivery can become long and difficult. Or the baby may be *premature*— born before the full nine months. In premature babies, the lungs or other parts of the body may not be fully developed. This can cause severe health problems and can require the baby to remain in the hospital much longer. It's important to realize that these things *can* happen. You and your girlfriend should have a plan ready in case of any complications during birth.

Preparing the House for Baby

Before you bring the baby home, you will need to shop for supplies and furniture. Maybe you have relatives or friends who can lend you some of the big items, such as a crib or stroller. If not, garage sales or thrift shops are good places to look. Here is a partial list of what you will need:

Furniture A full-size or porta-crib with a properly fitting mattress. Be sure your crib meets safety requirements. A waterproof pad helps keep the bed clean and dry. You'll also need a safe place to lay the baby down while you change its diapers.

Bringing baby home is an exciting moment for the family.

A small dresser with a wide top can double as a changing table and a place to store baby's clothes.

Baby carriers Car seats are required by law in many states. They are the best way to keep baby safe in a moving vehicle. A newborn will need an infant-size car seat. You may also want a pack for carrying baby on your back and a stroller.

Food The mother may decide to *nurse* your baby—feed it with milk from her breasts. If she chooses not to nurse, you will need to buy *formula* and nursing bottles from a store. Formula is a liquid like mother's milk. During the first few weeks, the only food most babies need is breast milk or formula. Breast-feeding is less expensive than bottle-feeding. But some mothers, especially those who are working or in school, find it hard to nurse their babies.

Diapers Cloth diapers can be washed and re-used. Although disposable diapers are meant to be thrown away for convenience, they are expensive and a problem for the environment.

Bath supplies It's very important to keep baby's head supported during baths. A big, thick piece of sponge in the sink or tub makes a good cushion. Some people like to bathe a newborn baby in a small plastic tub. You may also want to get baby powder, lotion, a mild shampoo, and soap.

Clothing Most babies stay in sleepers the first few months of life. One style is a nightgown with a drawstring in the bottom. Another is like pajamas with feet. You'll also need socks, undershirts, and bibs. For outside, dress the baby as warmly as you would dress. Don't forget a hat to keep sun and cold away from baby's head.

Receiving blankets These are small, soft, lightweight blankets. Infants like to be wrapped snugly in them.

Toys Babies like to look at brightly colored things that move. For an infant, objects that hang above the crib (like a mobile) are good.

A Change in Schedule

Remember, having a baby is hard work. Mom may still be weak and tired for a while. She'll need more help at first. Newborns need care 24 hours a day. Every few hours, day or night, it's feeding time. In between, the baby may need to be held, changed, rocked, and entertained.

Having a baby in the house changes everyone's schedule. There don't seem to be enough hours in the day. It's important for the two of you to share the duties around the house as well as taking care of the baby.

It may help to set up a schedule with the baby's mother. Decide who will care for the baby during which times of the day. This will give you a regular time with your child. If Mom is always the one who feeds, changes, or plays with the baby, your son or daughter may form a stronger bond with her than with you. This can make you feel like an outsider.

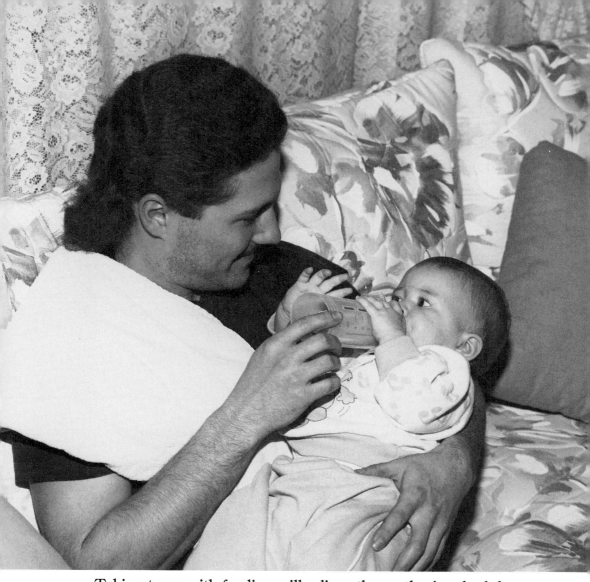

Taking turns with feeding will relieve the mother's schedule and add to the feeling of closeness for the father.

And it may cause problems between you and the baby's mother. You can learn to care for a new baby. It just takes a little practice and a lot of love.

Making room for a third person in your life is not easy, especially when that person needs constant attention. It's important to remember that Mom and Dad need time together without the baby. And each of you also needs time alone.

What If Baby's Home Is Not Your Home?

Darian wanted to help raise his son. But he and Shawna didn't want to get married. "We both lived with our parents. Since the houses weren't far apart, it was easy to share time with him. We agreed the baby would live with Shawna. During the day, she would go to school and I would keep him. Since I worked nights, that made things easy."

Darian bought the diapers and food he would need while the baby was at his house. Shawna bought supplies for her home. When a big expense like a doctor visit came along, they shared the cost.

Their baby is three months old now. "So far it's worked out great," they both agree. "We don't have to put him in day care, and we each get to watch him grow." But they realize that things could get more complex as he gets older. "When he starts needing *discipline*, for example, it will be hard for him if we each set different rules," Darian says. He's also worried about what would happen if either he or Shawna had to move. "It would be real tough only seeing him once in a while. I think about that a lot. I don't know what I'd do."

Darian and Shawna are able to talk and plan together what they think is best for their son even though they do not live together. They can express their feelings and concerns to each other. In the future this may help them make decisions for them and their child.

A father's guidance and support become more important as the child grows.

Chapter **8**

Fatherhood Is Forever

If you don't like your car, you can trade it for a different kind. When a husband and wife no longer love each other, they may decide to get divorced. But fatherhood is forever. Unless you choose adoption or abortion, your child is yours for the rest of your life. Even if you do not live together, your child is still your responsibility. If you accept that responsibility and do the best job you can of raising your child, he or she can be your finest reward.

Help in Becoming a Good Parent

Many parts of parenting may seem natural to you. No one will need to tell you to pick up the baby when it is crying. But there will be times when you won't know what to do.

How do you know if a child's stomach pains are serious enough to call the doctor? What do you do when your baby wakes in the middle of the night with a high fever? When should you begin toilet training? Is your child developing normally? These, and hundreds of other questions, have worried new parents for many generations.

For more than 50 years, millions of parents have turned to a book called *Baby and Child Care* by Dr. Benjamin Spock for practical advice. You can get this book in the library or buy it in a bookstore.

The book has chapters on a child's development at each age, from infancy through the teenage years. Thoughts about raising children have changed greatly in the last 50 years. So each time Dr. Spock's book is reprinted, new information is added to keep current with modern ideas.

Loving Your Child Once the Newness Wears Off

During the first few weeks, the responsibility and challenge of fatherhood are exciting. But after those first few weeks, the newness begins to wear off. The routine is the same day after day. Caring for your baby may not seem like fun any longer. You feel trapped. At times like these, it is important to remind yourself that things will get better. Each month you will notice how much the baby is growing and learning. You will enjoy some stages of your child's development more than others.

Sometimes it can be fun to include your child in activities you enjoy with your friends.

When fatherhood starts to seem like a burden, trying changing your routine. Even a small change can make a big difference. When you get tense, put the baby in the stroller and go for a walk. The fresh air and change of scenery may be good for both of you. Do something with your child that's fun for you, too, like taking a drive or spending an afternoon at the beach. Baby can fit into your life. You don't have to give up all your activities. Plan ahead when you want to include the baby in your fun. If you don't want to take the baby, leave it with someone responsible.

Controlling Your Anger

It's a proven fact that teenage parents are more likely to abuse their children than other parents. Teens have more trouble dealing with their emotions. Don't be a part of the child-abuse statistics. Learn how to recognize and control your anger.

There are times when *every* parent loses patience with a child. Babies can cry a lot, especially those who suffer from *colic*—sharp pains in the stomach and abdomen. Toddlers like to do things over and over after they have been told no. You may feel like screaming and striking back. *But never hit your child in anger.* If you are unhappy about your child's behavior, tell him or her how you are feeling and why. Let your children know what you expect from them. If you are in control, they may learn a better way to handle their own anger.

It is also true that parents who were abused when they were children are more likely to abuse their own kids. This means that if you were abused as a child, you have to try twice as hard to control your anger. You may not have been taught healthy ways to express how you are feeling. If you begin to feel angry, walk away, cool off, or call a friend for help. Give yourself time to think. Try to remember how scared you felt as a child when your mom or dad was hurting you.

Child abuse is on the rise in the United States. Parents are under increasing pressure. Our world is stressful. When you come home tired and cranky from working hard all day, the last thing you want to hear is a crying baby. Remind yourself that very young children do not *try* to be bad. They may need something they cannot express. Try holding your child, rocking it, taking it for a ride in the stroller, or talking quietly to it. It may take a few minutes. Be patient. Both you and the child will probably settle down. If you feel you have a problem controlling your anger when you are around your child, call Parents Anonymous (see page 61). This is an organization that helps people break the habit of child abuse. Trained counselors will talk with you. No need to feel embarrassed. They are there to help.

Setting a Good Example

Children learn by copying. A child learns to walk by watching other people walk. He or she learns to talk by listening to others and making the same kinds of sounds.

In the eyes of a child, Mom and Dad are probably the most important people in the world. As children begin the job of sorting out right from wrong, they look to their parents for answers. "Is it OK to hit someone when I'm mad?" If Dad does it, the child will probably decide it's OK. But if Dad keeps his temper and settles his argument by talking, the child may decide that this is the best way.

If you don't want your child to drink alcohol or use drugs, then look at your own behavior. If you

Time spent reading to your child is very special for both of you.

want your child to do well in school, let him or her know that you think education is important. Turn off the TV and pick up a newspaper or a magazine. Have books around your home and read to your child. What the child sees you doing, he or she may want to do, too. Children want to be like adults. They want to practice what you're doing. So you must be sure *you* are doing the right things!

As Your Child Grows Older

A father often finds that he becomes more important in his child's life as the child grows older. At first, the baby needs a lot of physical attention—feeding, changing, dressing, and cuddling. In many homes, Mom feels more comfortable doing these things for her new baby.

As your child gets older, you may find more ways for the two of you to be together. Time with Dad often seems more special to a young child, especially if you are away at work each day. Take time to enjoy your child and to have fun. Play ball, wrestle, go on picnics, take a walk, make dinner, watch movies together—whatever the two of you like to do. Even doing chores together can be fun. Children usually like to help. Chores like painting, fixing or washing the car, cutting the grass, or cleaning out the garage can teach kids how a family works together and shares responsibility.

Beating the Odds

It's not going to be easy. Statistics say the road is rough for teenage parents.

- Children born to parents under 17 are twice as likely to die as those born to other parents.
- The divorce rate for parents under 18 is three times greater than for those who have their first child after age 20.
- Fewer than 5 percent of single mothers receive any money from the baby's father.

Making a Wise Decision

Don't get forced into fatherhood. Before you become sexually active, think about the lifetime commitment you may be making. Be certain that you *want* to be a father. Be sure you understand what it takes to raise a child. Ask yourself honestly if you are willing to do it. Think about the things you probably will be giving up, like dating, partying, school, traveling, and the freedom to be on your own. Are you ready to tie yourself down? Are you ready to put the needs of your girlfriend or wife and your child first? Are you able to provide for your new family?

Even if you answer yes to these questions, there will be tough times. There are no easy routes for teenage dads. You must be willing to make sacrifices. You must be ready to work hard. Above all, you must commit yourself to raising your child, being there when you are needed.

Until now, there has been very little help for teen fathers who want to share in raising their children. Most programs have been geared to teen mothers. But slowly things are changing. The Responsive Fathers Program in Philadelphia is one of six new plans in the U.S. set up just for fathers.

Don't try to work through teen fatherhood alone. There is help. To find out more, turn to the agencies listed in the back of this book.

Glossary—*Explaining New Words*

abortion A natural or medical way of ending a pregnancy.

adoption Placing a child to live in a home other than that of its natural parents.

AIDS Acquired immunodeficiency syndrome, a sexually transmitted virus.

anesthetics Drugs given by a doctor to reduce or dull pain.

budget A plan for spending money.

cesarean birth The delivery of a baby by surgery.

condom A rubber casing rolled over an erect penis; a contraceptive.

delivery The stage of childbirth when the baby emerges from the mother's body.

fetus The unborn baby that is living in its mother's body.

GED General Equivalency Diploma; a diploma that is equal or "equivalent" to a high school diploma, for people who can no longer attend a regular high school.

immature Not grown-up; childish.

immune system Parts of the body that help to fight off diseases.

intercourse Sexual contact in which the penis enters the vagina.

Lamaze A method of delivery that helps mothers relax during childbirth using natural methods, without the help of drugs.

midwife A health-care person who is trained in the delivery of babies.

minimum wage The lowest rate of pay that the government allows employers to pay workers.

morals Beliefs about right and wrong ways of behavior.

moral support Help or encouragement in making decisions or getting through difficult times.

paternity Fatherhood; the condition of being a father.

pregnant Having unborn young growing inside a female body.

premature Happening too soon, before maturity or full growth.

prenatal Before birth.

trimester Each three-month period of pregnancy.

Where to Go for Help

Call one of these organizations to find out where to go for help in your town.

United Way
Planned Parenthood
Salvation Army
YMCA

Catholic Charities
Parents Without Partners
Your local hospital. Ask for
   "Adolescent Services."

Responsive Fathers Program
   In Philadelphia
      (215) 686-3910
   In Racine, Wisconsin
      (414) 554-1200
   In Fresno, California
      (209) 233-4500
   In Annapolis, Maryland
      (301) 659-7701
   In Cleveland, Ohio
      (216) 589-9675
   In Clearwater, Florida
      (813) 545-4511

Parents Anonymous
   1-800-421-0353

Boys Clubs of America
771 First Avenue
New York, NY 10017
(212) 351-5910
Ask about the program
called "SMART Moves."

National Organization on Adolescent Pregnancy and Parenting
4421-A East West Highway
Bethesda, MD 20814
(301) 913-0378

National Abortion Federation
1-800-772-9100

Catholics for a Free Choice
1436 U Street NW
Washington, DC 20009
(202) 986-6093

National Urban League
500 East 62nd Street
New York, NY 10021
(212) 310-9000
Their program called
"African American Adolescent
Male Development Center"
focuses on teen dads.

For Further Reading

Hughes, Tracy. *Everything You Need to Know about Teen Pregnancy*, rev. ed. New York: Rosen Publishing Group, Inc., 1992.
Answers such questions as "What is it like to be pregnant? What are my choices?"

Lindsay, Jeanne Warren. *Parents, Pregnant Teens, and the Adoption Option*. Buena Park, CA: Morning Glory Press, 1989. Focuses on the legal and emotional aspects of adoption.

Pennetti, Michael. *Coping with School Age Fatherhood*, rev. ed. New York: Rosen Publishing Group, Inc., 1988. Discusses teenage parenting from a father's viewpoint.

Richards, Arlene Kramer, and Willis, Irene. *What to Do If You or Someone You Know Is Under 18 and Pregnant*. New York: Lothrop, Lee & Shepard, 1983. Discusses in detail teen sex, birth control, pregnancy, childbirth, abortion, adoption, marriage, and babies.

Silverstein, Herma. *Teen Guide to Single Parenting*. New York: Franklin Watts, 1989. Tips on caring for your baby.

Spock, Benjamin. *Baby and Child Care*, rev. ed. New York: Dutton, 1985. A complete, day-to-day, practical guide for raising children.

Index

About the Author

Eleanor H. Ayer is the author of several books for children and young adults. She has written about people of the American West, World War II and modern Europe, and current social issues of interest to teenagers. Her recent topics include stress, depression, teen marriage, and teen suicide. Eleanor holds a master's degree from Syracuse University with a specialty in literacy journalism. She lives with her husband and two sons in Colorado.

Acknowledgments and Photo Credits

Cover photo by Chuck Peterson.
Photos on pages 20, 48, 53, 56: Stuart Rabinowitz; pp. 2, 9, 10, 17, 24, 28, 34, 38, 45, 50: Mary Lauzon.
Art on page 32 by Sonja Kalter.

Design/Production: Blackbirch Graphics, Inc.